DAVID BLAINE

Brandon Robshaw
and Rochelle Scholar

Published in association with The Basic Skills Agency

A MEMBER OF THE HODDER HEADLINE GROUP

The Publishers would like to thank the following for permission to reproduce copyright material:

Photo credits
p.2 © Nils Jorgensen/Rex Features; p.7 © Dave Allocca/DMI/Time Life Pictures/Getty Images; p.11 © D Herrick/DMI/Rex Features; p.15 © Rex Features; p.17 © Erik C Pendzich/Rex Features; p.20 © Charles Sykes/Rex features; p.24 © Rex Features.

Orders: please contact Bookpoint Ltd, 130 Milton Park, Abingdon, Oxon OX14 4SB. Telephone: (44) 01235 827720. Fax: (44) 01235 400454. Lines are open from 9.00–6.00, Monday to Saturday, with a 24-hour message answering service. Visit our website at www.hoddereducation.co.uk.

© Brandon Robshaw and Rochelle Scholar 2005
First published in 2005 by
Hodder Murray, a member of the Hodder Headline Group
338 Euston Road
London NW1 3BH

Impression number 10 9 8 7 6 5 4 3 2 1
Year   2010 2009 2008 2007 2006 2005

All rights reserved. Apart from any use permitted under UK copyright law, no part of this publication may be reproduced or transmitted in any form or by any means, electronic or mechanical, including photocopy, recording, or any information storage and retrieval system, without permission in writing from the publisher or under licence from the Copyright Licensing Agency Limited. Further details of such licences (for reprographic reproduction) may be obtained from the Copyright Licensing Agency Limited, of 90 Tottenham Court Road, London W1T 4LP.

Cover photo © Erik C Pendzich/Rex Features
Typeset in 14pt Palatino by SX Composing DTP, Rayleigh, Essex.
Printed in Great Britain by CPI Bath.

A catalogue record for this title is available from the British Library

ISBN-10 0 340 90060 1
ISBN-13 978 0 340 90060 4

Contents

		Page
1	The Glass Box	1
2	Early Life	4
3	Street Magic	6
4	More Tricks	9
5	Sadness and Success	12
6	More than Magic	14
7	Vertigo	18
8	Above the Below	21
9	Why?	26

1 The Glass Box

London 9.30pm on 5 September 2003.
Hundreds of people are standing
by the River Thames.
Thousands of people are watching on TV.
What do they see?
A young man climbing into a glass box.

When the young man is in the box
a crane lifts the box up.
The crane hangs the box over the River Thames.
The crowds cheer.
The man inside the box waves.
All he has with him is a mat,
a duvet, a pillow and a notebook.

David Blaine.

The man's name is David Blaine.
He is going to live in the glass box for 44 days.
He will not eat anything.
He will drink only water.
His body will starve.
He will be alone in the box.

David knows it is dangerous.
He tells a newspaper,
'Anything can go wrong
and I will have no way of knowing
until it is already too late.'

So why is he doing it?

2 Early Life

David Blaine was born in Brooklyn,
New York, on 4 April 1973.
When he was four years old
he saw a subway performer do a card trick.
'Wow!' thought David.
'I want to do tricks like that.'

He asked his mother to buy him some cards.
He practised with the cards alone in his room.
Soon he had learned his first trick.
He called all his family into the room.

'Watch this,' he said.
'This trick is called Pencil through the Card.'
He pushed a pencil right through a card.
Or that's what it looked like.
Then he showed the card.
There was no hole in it.

His family clapped.
'That's great!' said his mum.
'Well done!'

David liked being clapped and cheered.
He carried on practising.
He learned more and more tricks.
When he learned a new trick,
he always showed his family.
His mother always clapped the loudest.

When David was 17, he did acting classes.
He did well.
He even got some work in daytime TV dramas.

But acting was not what he really wanted to do.
His real love was magic.
He knew a lot of tricks by now.
He was good.
But how could he get noticed?
Then David had an idea.
He would do street magic.

3 Street Magic

David's idea for street magic was very simple.
He just stopped people on the street
and showed them tricks.
He wasn't dressed up like a magician.
He wore a black woolly hat,
cargo trousers and a T-shirt –
New York grunge style.
And his tricks were amazing.

Here's one of his tricks:
David stops a man on a New York Street.
He shows him a pack of cards.
'Pick a card,' he says.
'Any card.'

The man is surprised.
He takes out a card and looks at it.
A small crowd has gathered to watch.

David performing a card trick.

David puts the card back in the pack.
Then he throws the pack at a shop window.
All the cards fall to the ground.
Except one.
The ace of hearts.
It is stuck to the window.
On the inside.

'Was that your card?' asks David.
The man nods.
He is too surprised to speak.
The crowd is amazed.
How did David do it? It seems impossible!

That wasn't David's only trick.
Here's another one:
David stops another passer-by.
He asks the woman to tell him
the name of her best friend.
Just then a yellow taxi drives past.
It has the name 'Dawn' on it.
Dawn is the best friend's name.

The woman is so amazed she can't stop laughing.
How did he do it?

4 More Tricks

David carried on doing street magic for a while.
His tricks were so amazing,
people would give him money.

In one trick, David stops a passer-by
and asks him the time.
The man looks at his watch.
The hands on the watch speed up and whizz round.
The man can't believe it.
How did David do it?

In another trick,
David passes a beggar on the street.
The beggar's cup fills to the top with coins.
The beggar is amazed and delighted.
But how did David do it?

The trick that really freaks people out
is when David seems to rise up in the air.
He spreads out his arms and rises up.
His feet don't seem to touch the ground.
It looks as if he is floating
five centimetres above the ground.
The crowd gasps and screams.
It must be a trick.
He can't really be floating – can he?

David Blaine with his girlfriend, Manon von Gerkan.

5 Sadness and Success

In 1994, when David was 21 years old,
his mother died.
David was heartbroken.

His mother had always supported him.
She knew his goals and dreams.
Now David knew he had to succeed.
He had to succeed for her sake.

He worked even harder at his street magic.
He began to get well known.
He hired himself out as an entertainer,
doing tricks at parties.

Soon, he was invited to celebrity parties.
Madonna and Mike Tyson watched
as he did his magic.
They were amazed.
David became friends with
Leonardo DiCaprio and Robert de Niro.

He was getting somewhere.
But this wasn't enough.
He wanted to reach more people.
He wanted his own TV show.

Then David had an idea.
He took a video camera out
on to the streets of New York.
He filmed himself doing his street magic.
He sent the film to ABC TV in New York.

ABC TV rang him up the next day.
They loved the video.
They asked David to come and meet them.
'We like your style,' they said.
'Show us what you can do.'

David spread out his arms
and seemed to float off the ground.
They could not believe their eyes.

ABC TV gave David a million dollar contract.
This was in 1997.
The TV show was called
'David Blaine: Street Magic'.

6 More than Magic

David Blaine's first TV show
was a great success.
Two years later David did another show
called 'David Blaine: Magic Man'.

To promote this show, he did something strange.
It wasn't a magic trick.
David wanted to do something different.
Something that would test his mind and body.
An endurance test.
He had himself put into a glass coffin
under a tank of water.
And he stayed there, underwater,
for a whole week.
When he came out he had lost 11 kilograms
(24 pounds).

It was a strange thing to do.
But it got him noticed.
People could not stop talking about it.

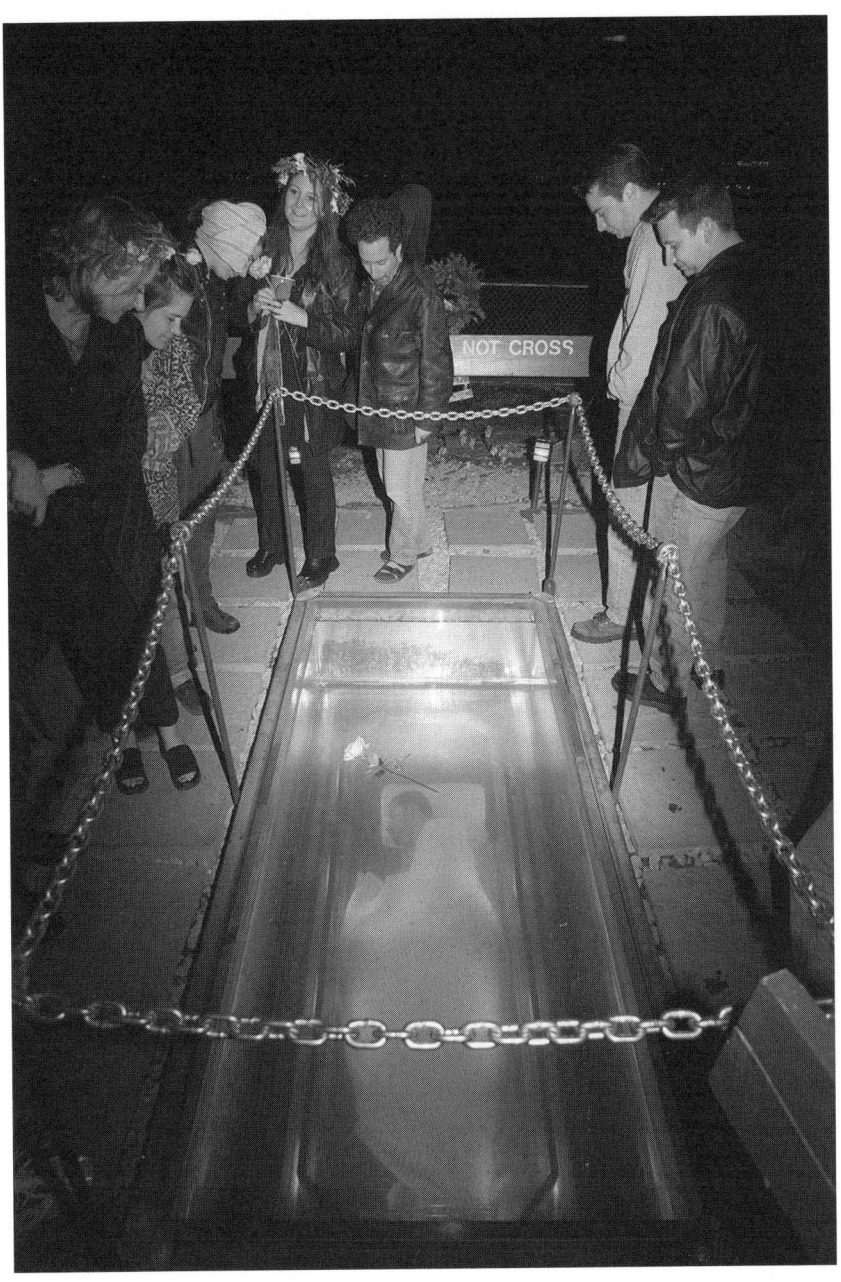

David in the glass coffin, underwater, where he stayed for a week.

The TV show 'David Blaine: Magic Man'
was another great success.
But now David wanted to do more
than just magic tricks.
He wanted to push his body to the limit.

In 2000, he did another endurance test.
He called the test 'David Blaine: Frozen in Time'.

Again David buried himself.
This time it was in a block of ice.
He stood frozen in Times Square, New York.
He stayed there for 58 hours.
Thousands of people came to see him.
Many people came to support him.
Others thought he was crazy.

It seemed that David wanted
to push himself to the limit.
Just how much can the human body and mind take?

David buried in a block of ice in Times Square, New York.

7 Vertigo

In May 2002, David was at it again.
He did another TV show.
To promote the show
he did another endurance test.
He called it 'David Blaine: Vertigo'.

David stood on a small platform.
The platform was on top of a tall pillar.
It was 30 metres from the ground.

Crowds gathered below to watch.
If David lost his balance,
he would fall 30 metres.
He would be smashed to pieces.

David stood on the platform for 35 hours,
without food,
without sleep.

He ended the stunt by diving off the platform
into a pile of cardboard boxes.
The crowd cheered.

But this still wasn't enough for David.
He wanted to push himself further.
He began planning another endurance test.

This one was to be called 'Above the Below'.
He was going to spend 44 days
alone in a glass box.
And he was coming to London to do it.

David on top of the pillar for his 'Vertigo' stunt.

8 Above the Below

London, September 2003.
David is alone in his glass box –
watching the people watching him.
People come day and night.
Sometimes they sing to him.
David waves.
The crowds cheer.

A jazz band comes and plays to him.
Breakdancers dance for him.
David stands up in his box.
He claps and thanks the people for their support.

But not everyone supports him.
When David did his stunts in New York,
the crowds were friendly.
In London, not everyone likes
seeing David Blaine in his glass box.

'What about all the starving
people in the world, David?'
shouts someone in the crowd.
David smiles at the man.
'Well, go do something about it.
Go help them. Give them some money.
Don't come and shout at me.'

Some people think David's a show-off.
They shout and swear at him.
Some people throw things.
After a few days, the glass box
has to be raised higher,
to keep it out of harm's way.

Somebody sends a radio-controlled
helicopter up to the box.
In the helicopter is a cheeseburger.
It hovers just outside
the glass walls of the box.
David laughs.

By week three, 20,000 people
have come to see David in his glass box.
David is finding it hard.
He is weak.
He says he has a sweet taste in his mouth.
He can taste pear drops.
He is starving.

David says he is learning
about himself in the box.
He is learning about the power of the mind.

On day 31 David writes,
'I feel like the walls are pushing into my head.'
Most of the time he is sitting
or lying down.
He feels dizzy when he stands up.

He has mood swings.
His skin looks patchy.

David suspended in his glass box above the River Thames in London.

On day 44, thousands of people
crowd by the River Thames.
They are waiting to see David
come out of the box.
His fans say he is a genius.
Others say he's a show-off.

The door of the box opens.
David stands.
He is thin and looks ill.
He is crying.
He says to the crowd,
'I've learned more in that little box
than I have in years.
I've learned how strong we all are
as human beings.'

9 Why?

Why does David Blaine do it?

He is a brilliant magician.
But why does he put himself through
these endurance tests?

Maybe he wants to show
what will power can do.
Maybe he wants to show people
how much our bodies and minds can stand.

Or does he just like being looked at?

He says he wants to be
the greatest showman of all time.
He makes a lot of money.
He made six million dollars in 2003.
He says, 'I'm not greedy at all.
I need a salary to continue doing what I do.'

Do his endurance tests
show how strong human beings can be?
Or are they just pointless?
Is David Blaine a show-off – or a genius?